Beautiful Bugs

A Coloring Book by Laura Maxwell

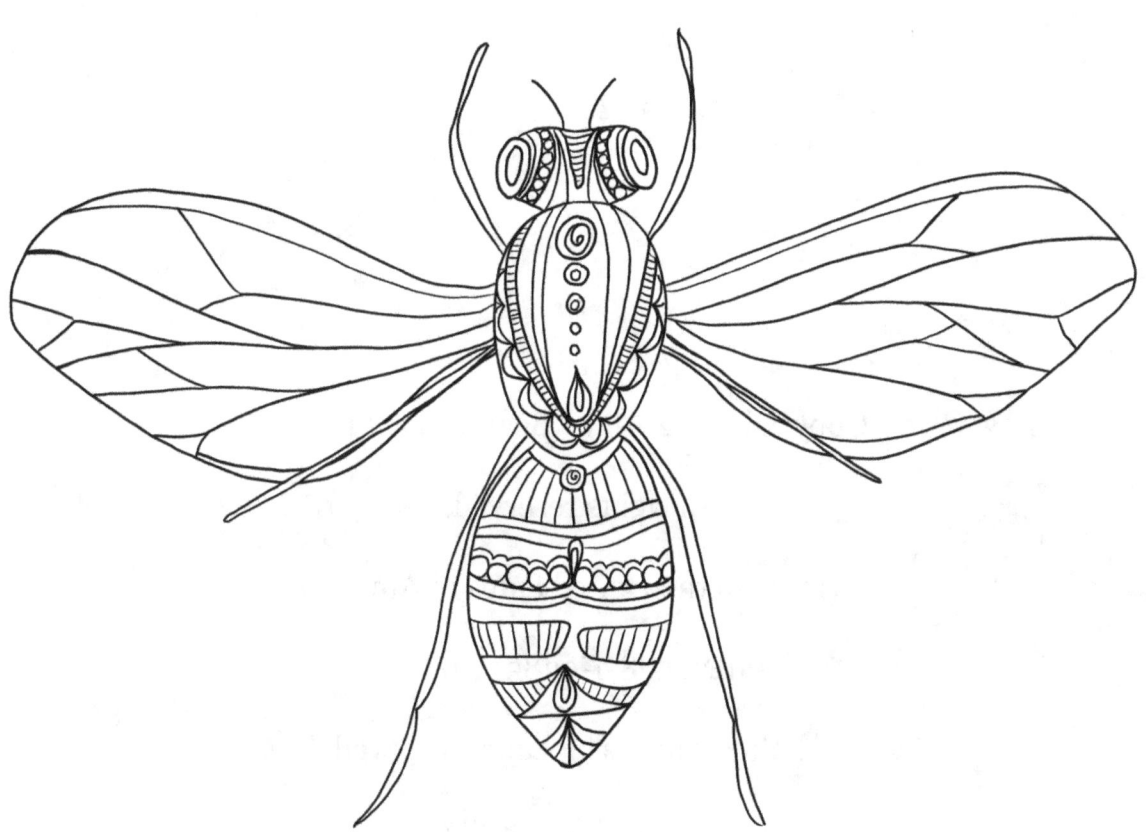

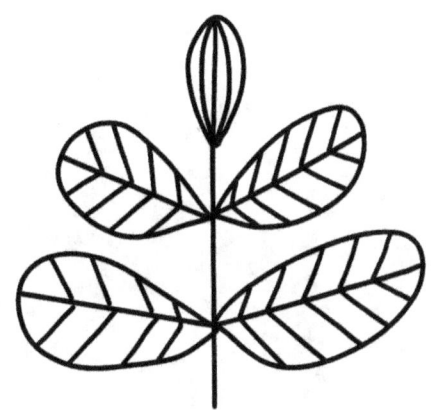

This book belongs to . . .

_____

a word from the artist...

In your hands is my very first coloring book. Each page in this book involved hours, days, and weeks of planning, drawing, and editing. Each bug was drawn by hand with pen and paper, and then edited on my computer. It was a labor of love and frustration. I'm so proud and excited that it has finally landed here, in your possession.

My hope is that you will find inspiration and relaxation through adding life to my drawings. This is a collaboration between you and me — I draw and you color. I'd love to see what you've down with my bugs! Please visit me at www.LauraKMaxwell.com.

—Laura

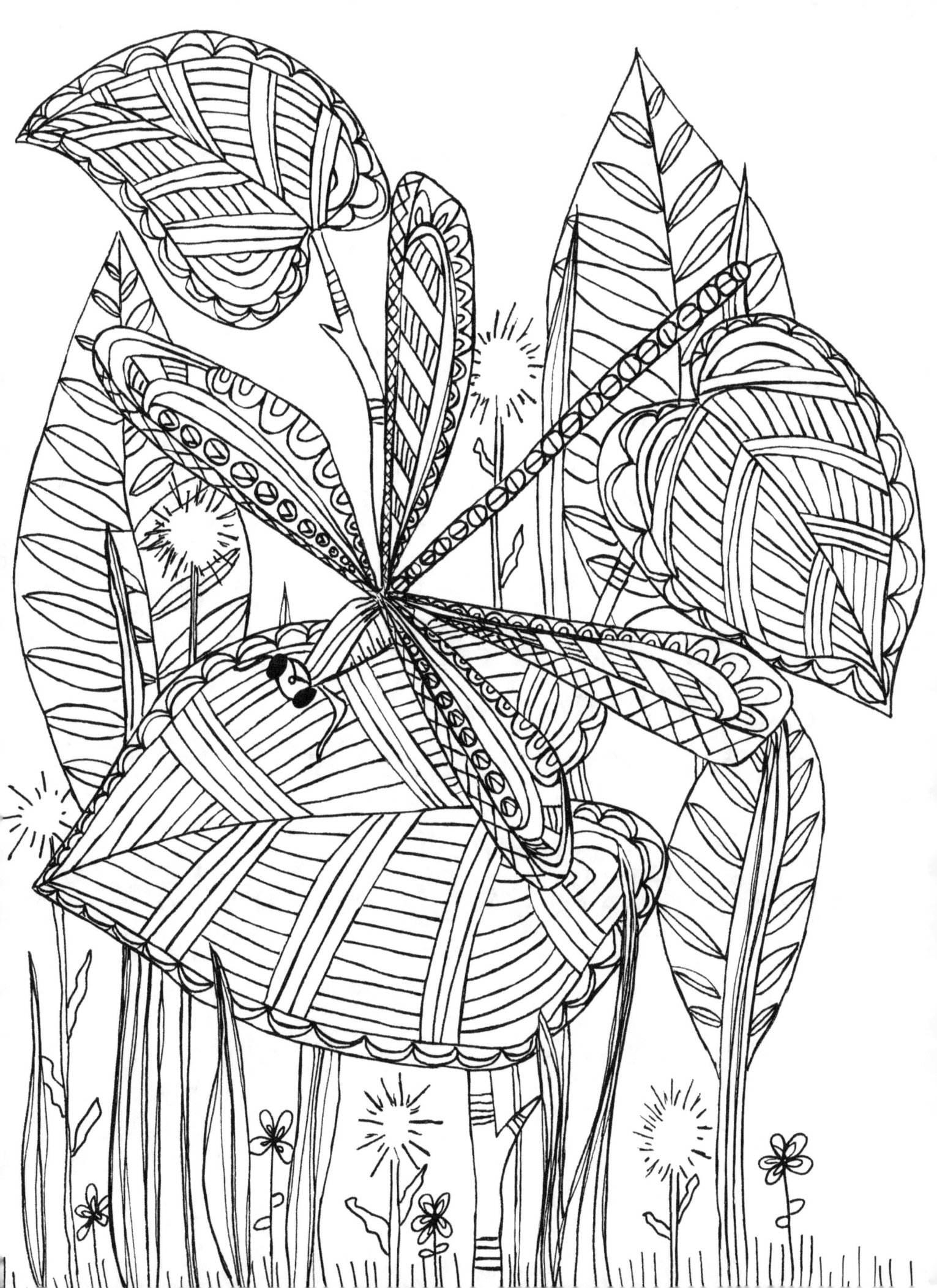

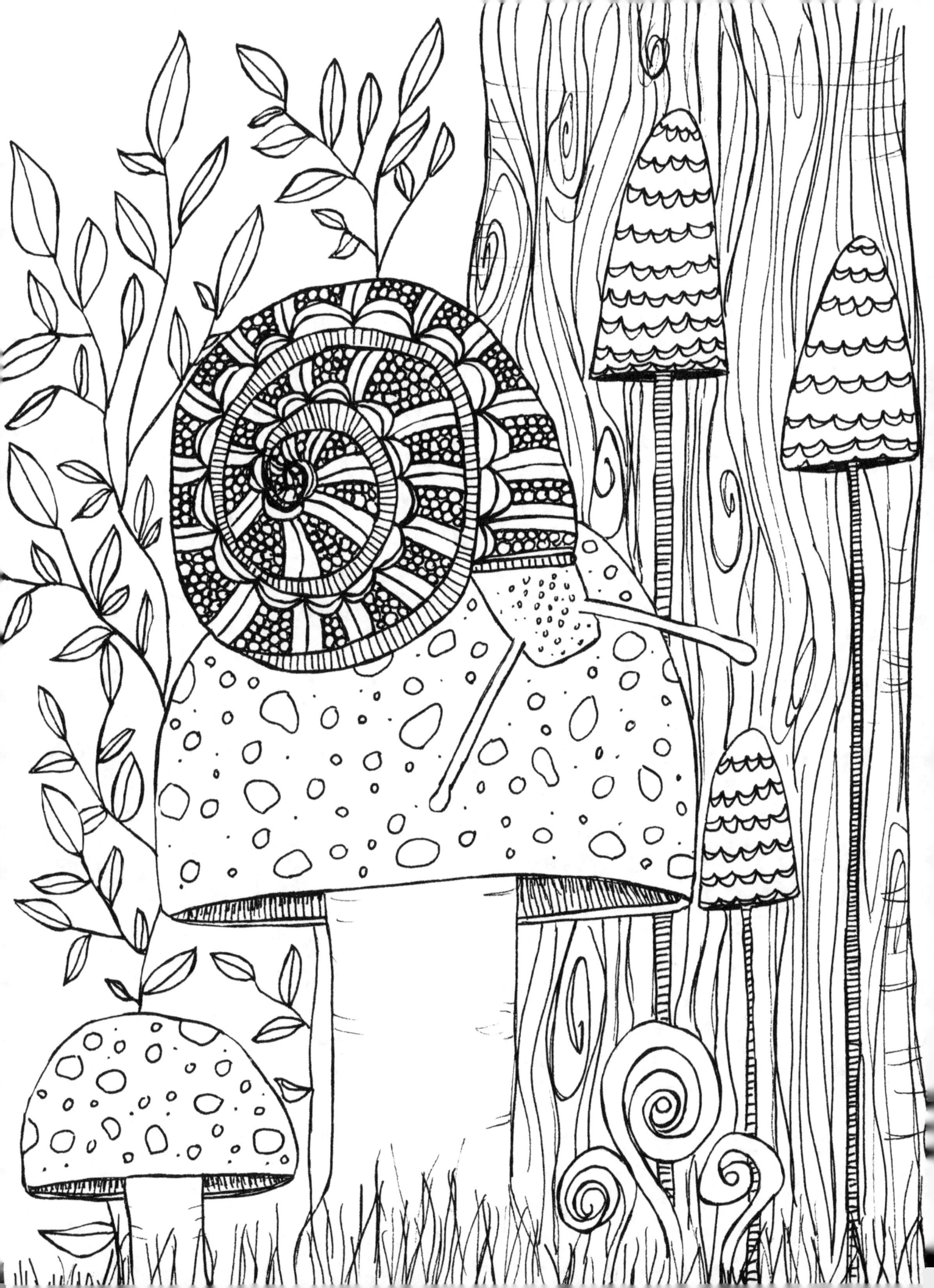

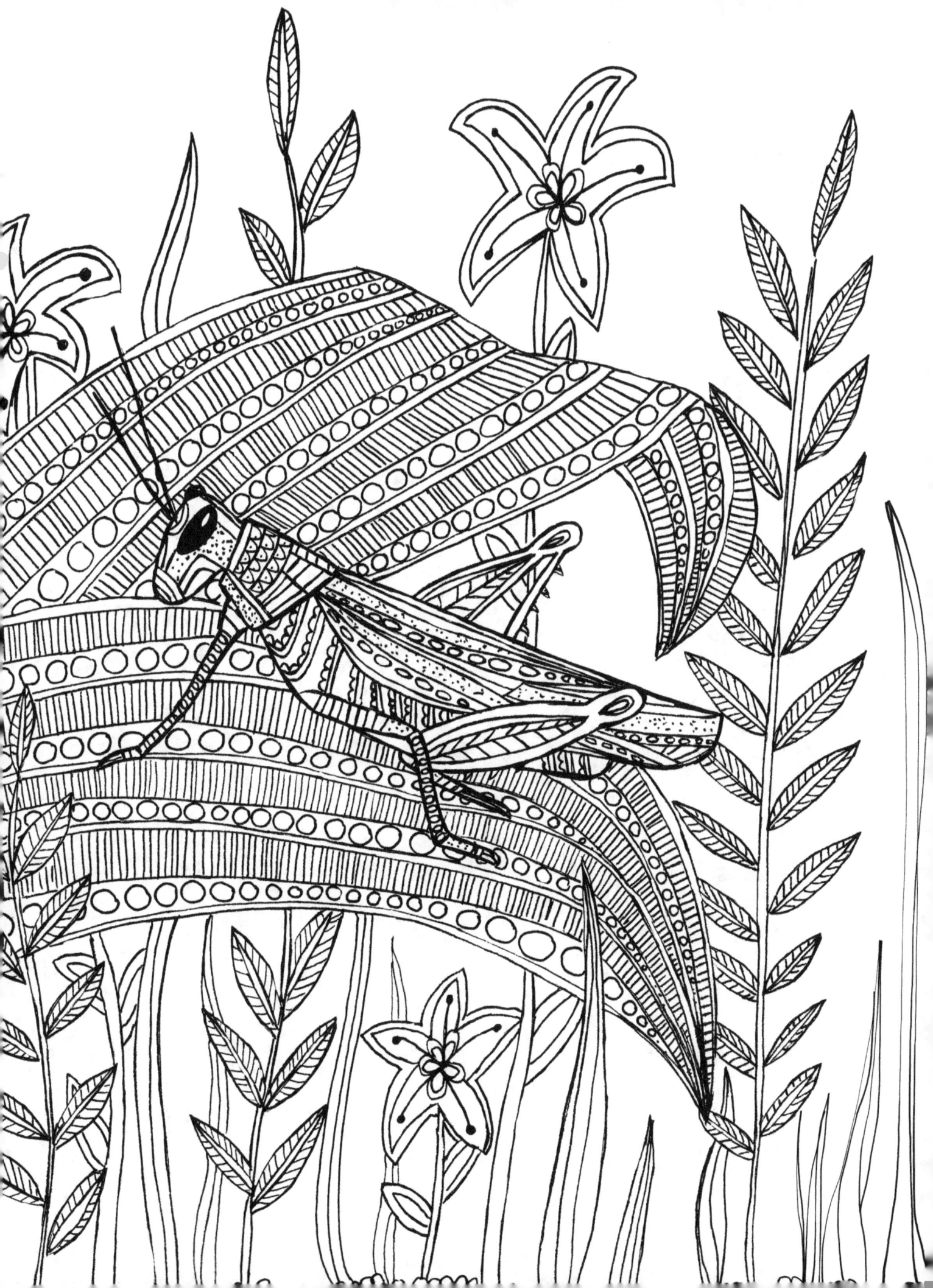

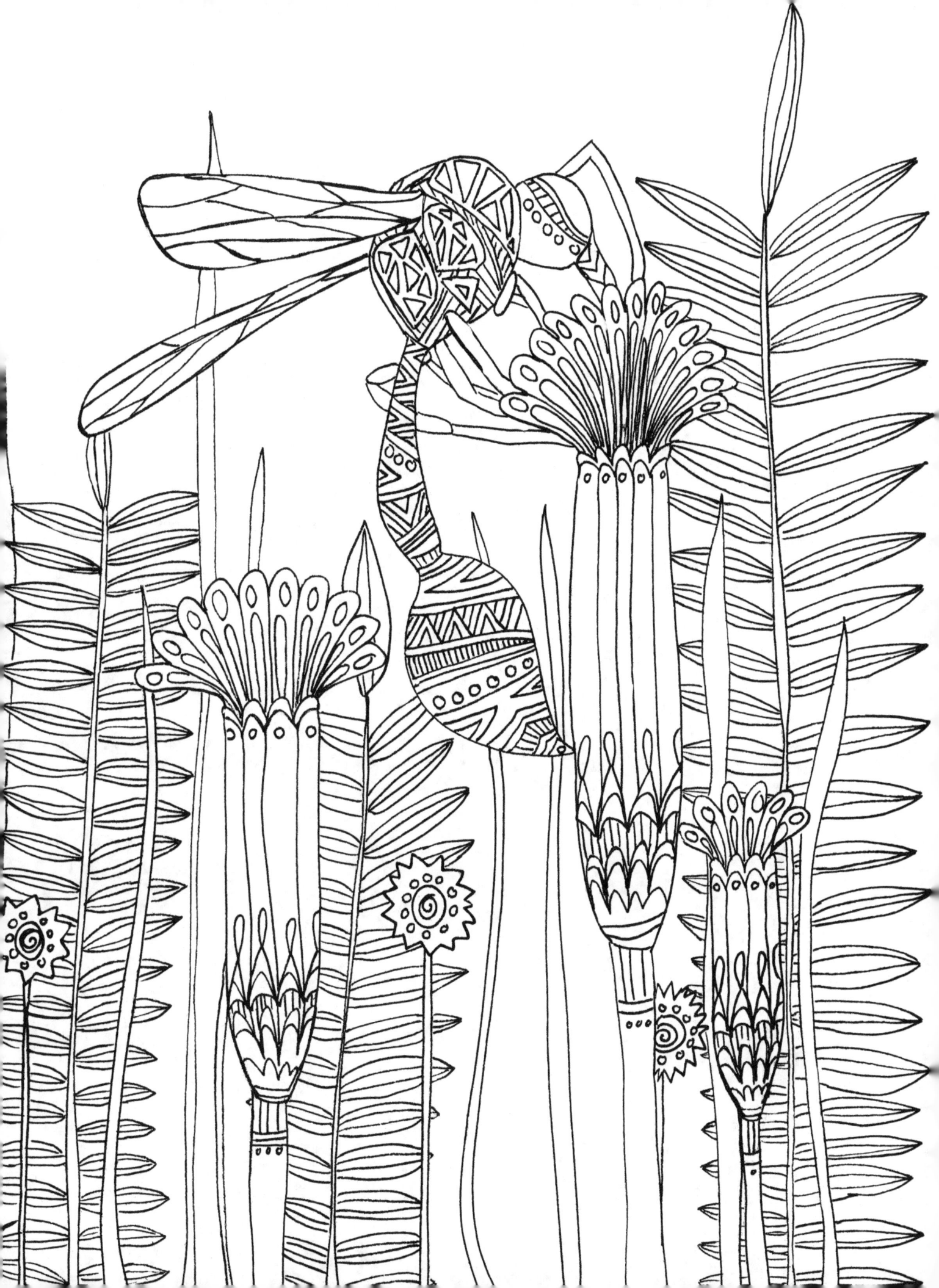

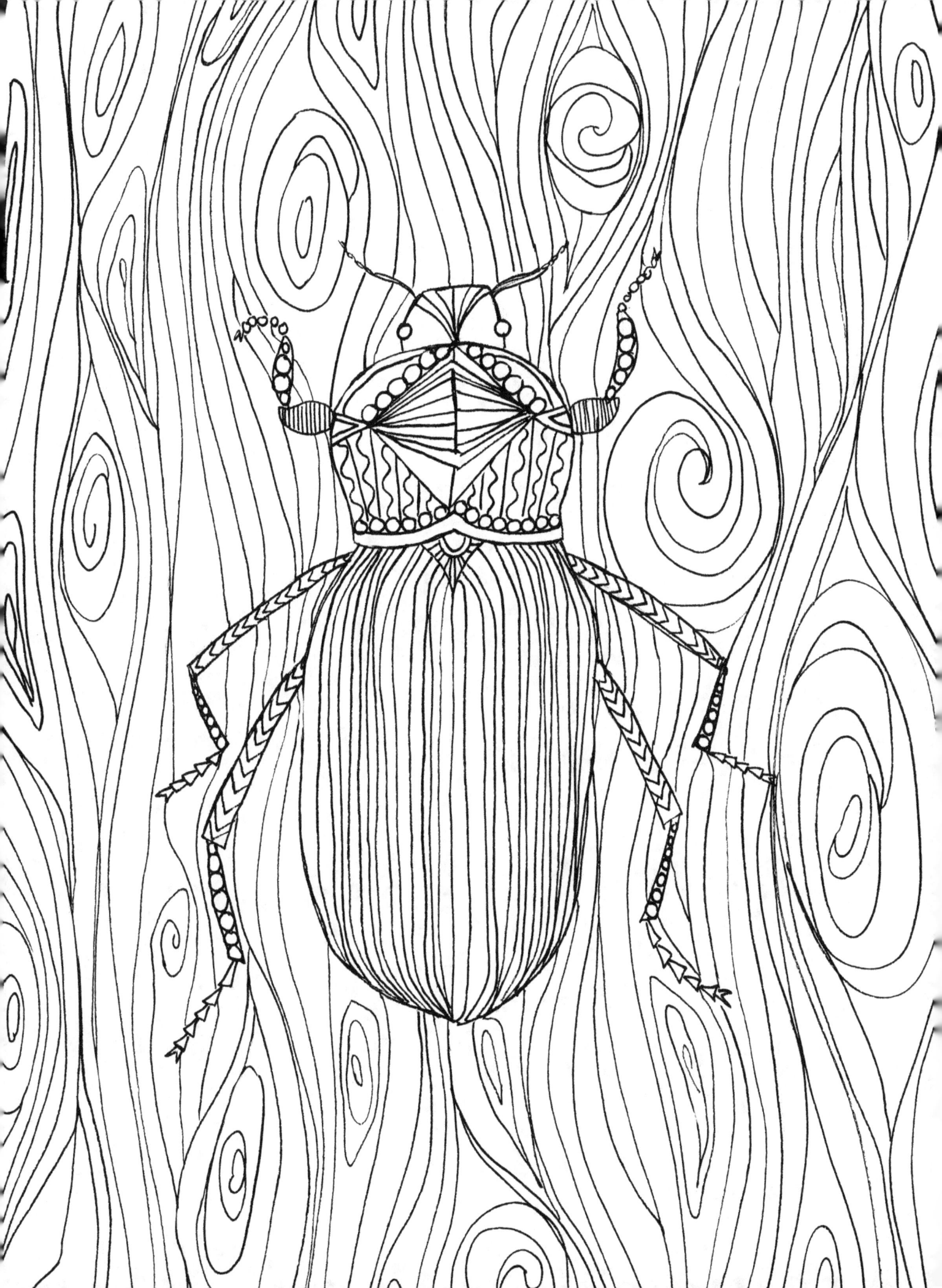

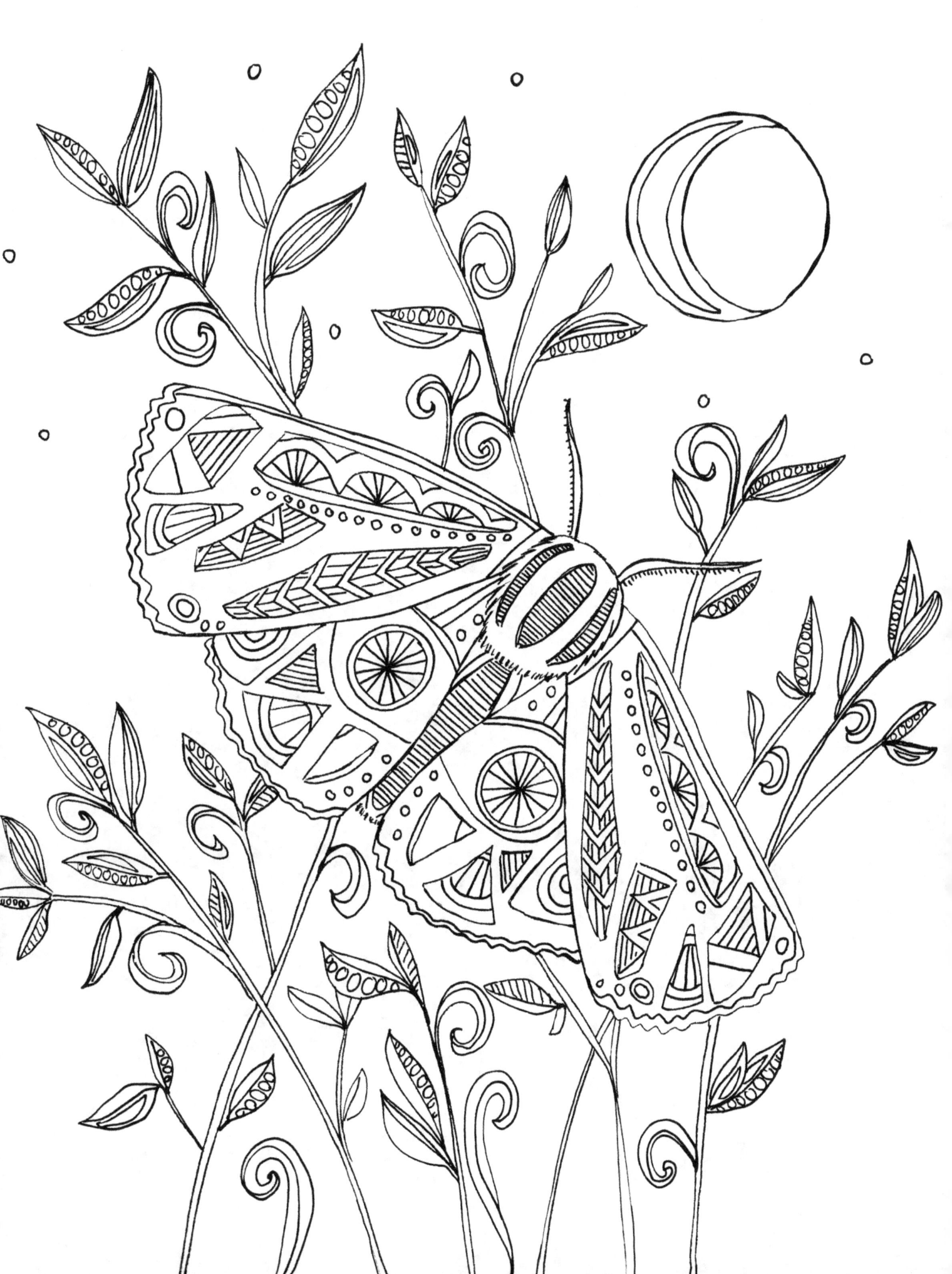

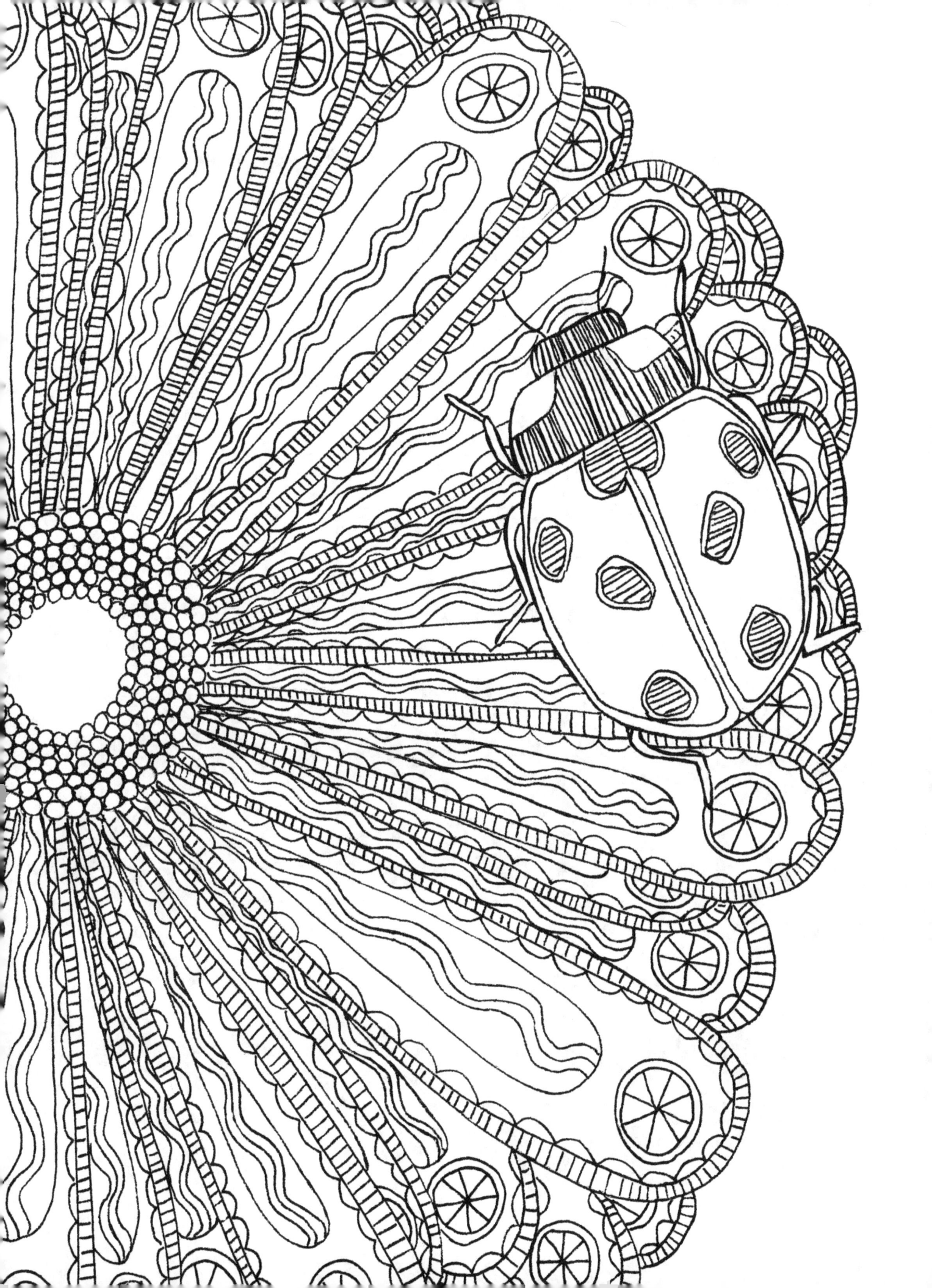

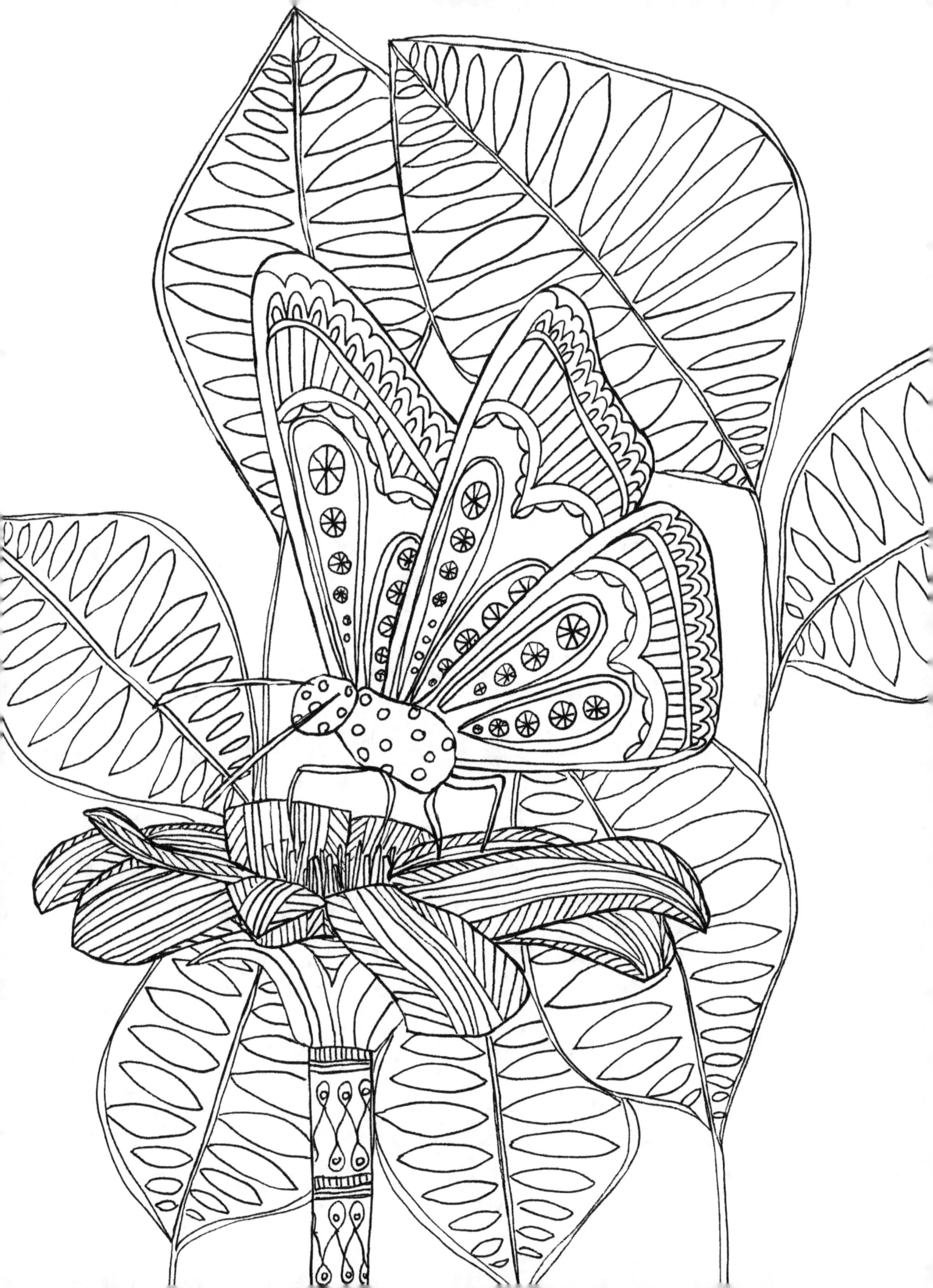

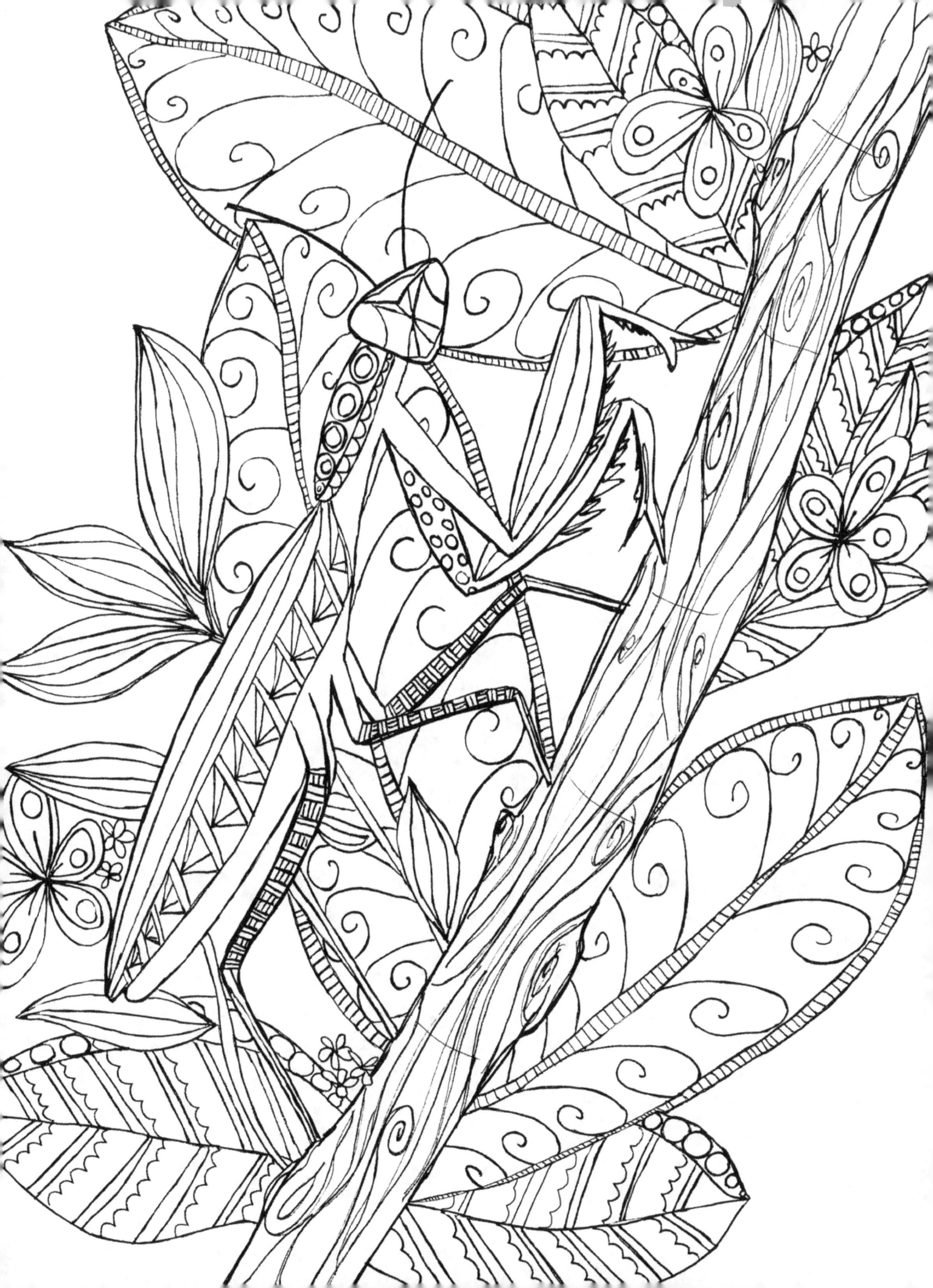

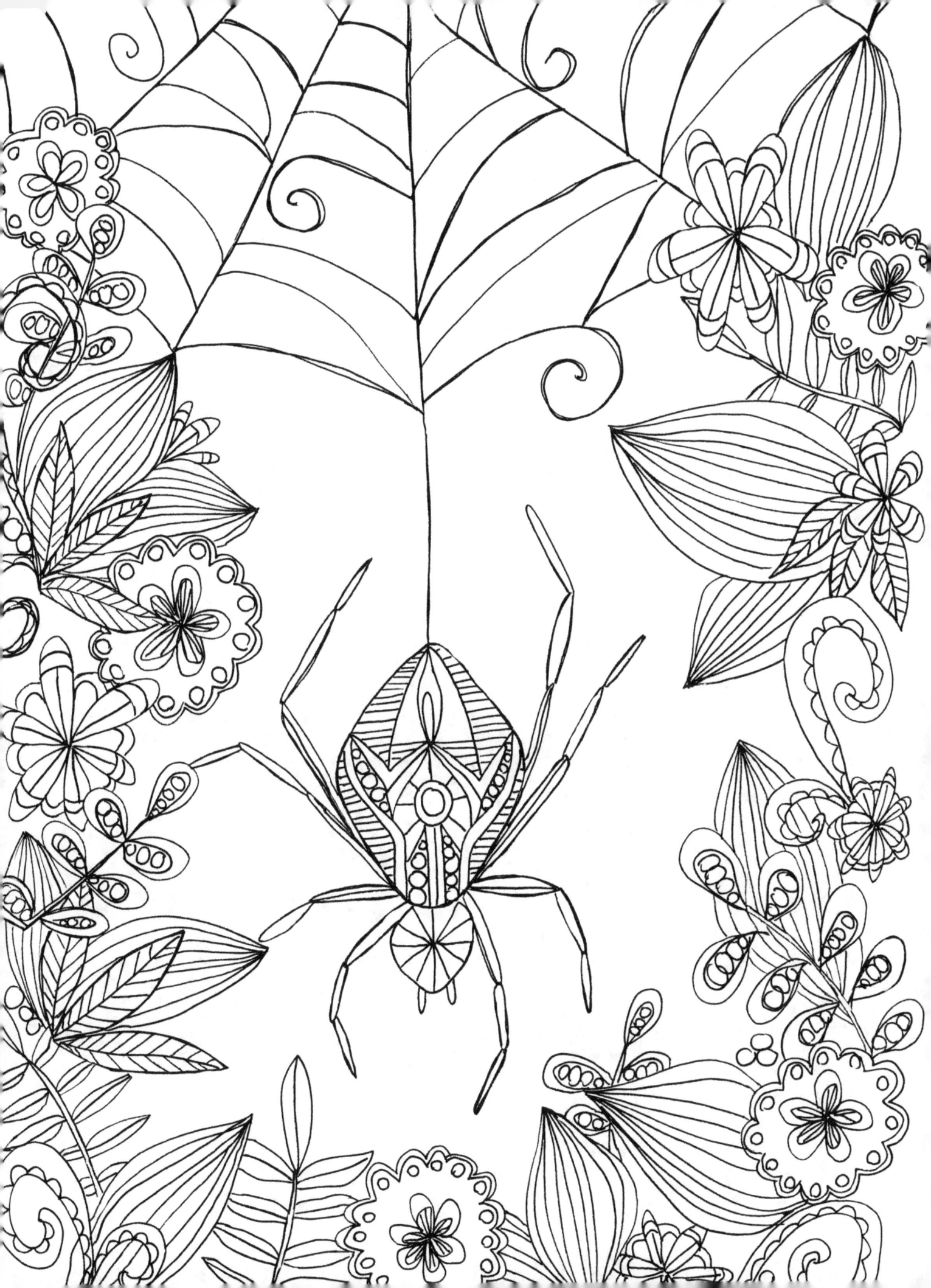

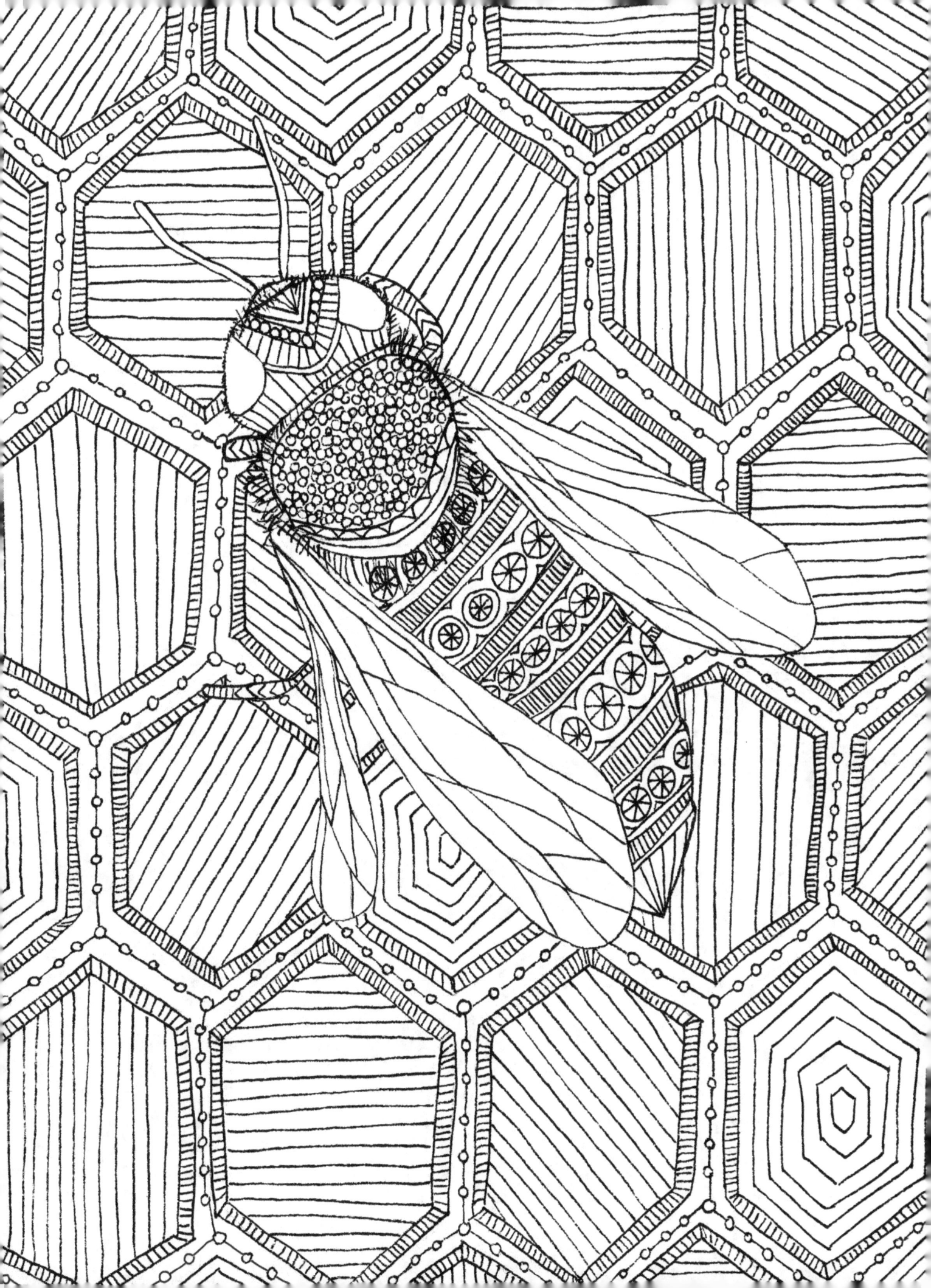

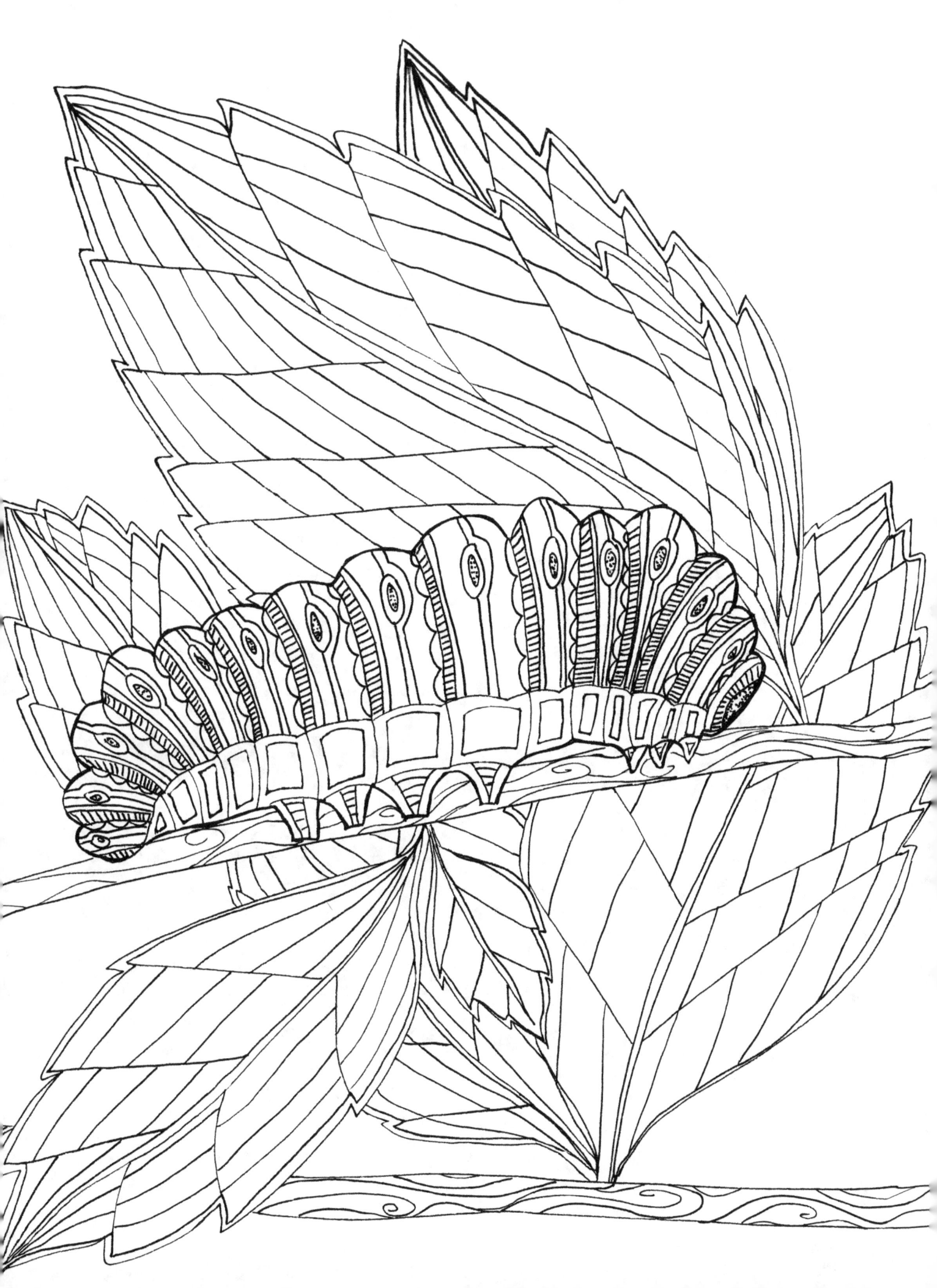

www.ingramcontent.com/pod-product-compliance
Lightning Source LLC
Chambersburg PA
CBHW081650220526
45468CB00009B/2608